How to Keep A GOOD MAN

5 SECRETS TO KEEPING THE MAN YOU LOVE

RODNEY D. ROBERTSON

Impact|Publishing
Impacting your world with inspiration™

How to Keep A GOOD MAN

Copyright © 2008 by Rodney D. Robertson

Unless otherwise indicated, Scripture quotations are taken from the *King James Version* of the Bible.

Scripture quotations marked (NLT) are taken from the *Holy Bible*, New Living Translation, copyright © 1996. Used by permission of Tyndale House Publishers, Inc., Wheaton, IL 60189. All rights reserved.

The author has emphasized some words in Scripture quotation in bold and italicized type.

ISBN 13: 978-0-615-18698-6
Printed in the United States of America.

Published by:
Impact Publishing, LLC
Baton Rouge, LA 70874

Cover/Interior design by:
www.r2design.com

CONTENTS

DEDICATION

*THIS BOOK IS DEDICATED TO my wife LaKeida
who practices divine wisdom and not the use of schemes,
tricks, and manipulation in order to keep me, her good man.
You are a great wife, lover, friend, and partner. I am
glad to be spending my life with you.*

YOUR GOOD MAN,
RODNEY

INTRODUCTION

A GOOD MAN IS HARD to find and in this day and time a good man is a rare commodity. Some women, out of desperation, have chosen to use tricks, schemes, love potions, and manipulation to keep a good man. It does not have to be like this. There are other principles and methods that can be used to keep the good man that God has blessed you with in your life.

In this book, I want to share with you five secrets on *How to Keep a GOOD Man* and practical love solutions to help improve your love-relationship so that you can experience a lasting connection with your good man. Even if you are a single woman in waiting, you can glean from these love secrets and be equipped to satisfy and *keep your good man* that is on the way. No matter what your race, religion, and economical status, if you are a woman who is committed to the man you love, you can benefit from this book. Inside this treasure chest, you will find golden nuggets to keeping and satisfying your good man.

No matter if he is the president of a thriving company or a waiter at a local restaurant, these practical love solutions will work if you work them and you will see an incredible transformation in your love-relationship and your GOOD man. So I implore you to continue reading and discover the secrets of *How to Keep A GOOD Man.*

CHAPTER ONE

Love Him

One thing you and I can agree on is that everyone wants to be loved. Whether your good man is strong and muscular or slim and conservative, he wants to be loved by you. Your good man is longing for that respect, sexual satisfaction, companionship, and acceptance by his spouse.

Love is a decision. Though the decision to love may produce good feelings; it is a decision. Love is not a feeling or goose bumps. It is a decision. It is a decision to accept him and see into him without judging him. It is a decision to provide the assurance of relational security. It is a decision to communicate to him "I am here for you". It is a decision not to be self-seeking but to consider and anticipate the needs of others. This is love.

Love is a verb and many times before love is felt; it can be seen through actions. You can say I love you all day long, but if you never express or convert your verbal love into actions; it remains only words. It is words plus actions that communicate clearly the message of love.

The power of love is demonstrated by action. *Love in action is doing the right thing, at the right time, with the right motive.* It is your love in action that will win him over and cause him to draw closer to you. It is your actions that cause him to not only hear your sweet words, but to feel the impact of your love.

You can make a lasting difference in your love-relationship and I want to help you do just that. Here are some basic love needs that every good man has and if you meet them, your love relationship will go to another level in intimacy and fulfillment.

#1 SEXUAL SATISFACTION

Yes ladies, your good man needs sexual satisfaction. Just as you have a real need for an emotional connection, he has a real need for sexual satisfaction. For a man, having sexual intercourse is his way of connecting with you intimately. This need for sexual satisfaction is a real need and if you are not willing to meet that need; you leave the door open for the office secretary, Ms. Available and whoever else to come in and meet the need of your good man.

You, as the wife, monitor the sexual temperature in your home. If your attitude toward lovemaking is negative, your husband will not be so eager to draw close to you. Even if he does, he will only come to get his sexual tension relieved and will not even consider your need for sexual healing.

One thing is for sure, if he is a good man, he will not continually push himself on someone who is not responding favorably. If there is no interest, you as his wife will receive no response from him.

At this point, sexual frustration builds up within him like red-hot lava rising in a volcano. An attractive lady happens to come along and offers a listening ear to his frustrations. Then, his mind is bombarded with the enticing thoughts of the enemy. Thoughts such as, "*She understands you. She listens to you. Your wife doesn't care about you or what you need.*" It is these thoughts that are presented to the mind of your husband, and if he does not fear God and respect his commitment to you; he may enter the door opened for adultery and a broken marriage just to experience bliss and a momentary tension relief.

It is your breasts that should satisfy him at all times (see Proverbs 5:19) and not the lady in the office, down the street, or around the corner in the neighborhood. It is you he wants. So take the time and learn what he likes. Ask him what he likes (never assume). *Make a decision to be desirable.* Fix yourself up. Take out the rollers. Visit Victoria Secrets and begin to prepare yourself for love making mentally, emotionally, and physically.

#2 RESPECT

Your good man needs respect. Aretha Franklin said it best, "R-E-S-P-E-C-T find out what it means to me". It is very important for you as a wife to find out what respect means to your husband. Respect carries a lot of weight for a man and when he is not respected; he will not stay around.

In Ephesians 5:33, God commands the man to love his wife as he loves himself and that the wife respects her husband. To the man and woman, it is not a matter of if your spouse deserves it or not, but it is a command from the heavenly Father. Husband love your wife! Wife respect your husband!

Another word for respect is honor. Every good man wants to be honored. Honor means high regard or respect. Honor in its verb form means to respect greatly and to show high regard for. In the life of your good man, he wants to be respected greatly and highly regarded. He may not verbally communicate it to you, but I assure you that he wants to be HONORED. If you do not honor him, you will not be able to effectively love, praise, support or listen to him.

When someone is being honored, another is recognizing his worth. It is the responsibility of a good man's family and friends to discern or recognize his worth and the role he plays in the relationship. Honor says to the person being honored that "I am valuable to you." Again, respect your good man.

#3 Acceptance without Condemnation

Acceptance is very important to us as men. When your husband decides to be open and honest, he wants to know that he will be heard and not judged. He also wants to know that what he shares with you won't be used against him and thrown in his face six months or sixty seconds later. He wants to be accepted based upon his character and the contents of his heart. Don't judge him based upon his past, present or future mistakes. Accept him. See into him with eyes of love and approval.

#4 FRIENDSHIP

He needs friendship. He desires for you to walk with him through life and make living more pleasant and worthwhile. He longs for you to walk with him in the same direction sharing in his passion and interests. He longs for friendship. Are you his friend? Would he call you friend or is he sleeping with the enemy? Be his friend and not his opponent.

LOVE *in* ACTION

- ⊙ Purposely show him your love with words and actions.
- ⊙ Ask him what he likes (Never assume).
- ⊙ Accommodate his desires.
- ⊙ Listen to him without judging him.
- ⊙ Respect him and the role he plays in your life and family.
- ⊙ Whatever your task, do it with all your heart out of reverence for God.

QUESTIONS *of the* HEART:

What did I learn from Secret 1 *Love Him*?

How can I implement this secret beginning today?

NOTES

CHAPTER TWO

Praise Him

The second secret I give you to keeping a good man is to praise him. I know that sounds simple, but it is a powerful tool that will get your good man motivated and ready to take on the world. In your mouth, my sister, is the power to build up or tear down a man's esteem, dreams, and his desire to even come home to you.

One word from you can either repel or attract him to you. The Bible says that death and life are in the power of the tongue and those who love it shall eat the fruit of it (see Proverbs 18:21). The words you're speaking to your good man are either killing him or supplying him with life, refreshment, hope, confidence, peace and the list goes on.

Now, the question is, what have you been saying to your good man lately? Is he encouraged when he leaves your presence or discouraged? Does he feel confident and strong when he leaves your presence or does he feel defeated and weak? When he leaves your presence, does he feel like a kid or a king? You, his spouse, are the first person who has the opportunity to influence him with your words. Sometimes it may appear like he is ignoring you, but trust me; he is listening. He is taking in the words of the one who says she loves him, whether they are negative or positive.

A GOOD WORD

A word spoken in due season or at the right moment is good (see Proverbs 15:23). For example, when my wife and I were living in an apartment, I would get off from work much earlier than she would. Because I came home first, I would cook, clean and do the laundry. Well one particular day, I did not feel appreciated about all the work I was doing, so I decided to verbalize my complaint. Now let me say that feelings are neither wrong nor right; they are just feelings. However, they should be expressed in the most tactful way. So I went to my wife, expressed myself, and she heard me.

Little did I know God had given LaKeida a power phrase for me that I will never forget. She came in the next day after hearing my complaint and said, "Baby I appreciate you for cooking, cleaning, and doing the laundry after working hard all day. You are the *Laundry King*." I heard every word she said, but when she said you are the "*Laundry King*" something within me rose up and I felt good about what I was doing. I was the *Laundry King* and what that meant to me was nobody could do the laundry like me. In fact, LaKeida never heard me complain again about doing the laundry or any other task because I was the *Laundry King*.

Now to keep it balanced, I must also tell you that God corrected me. He reminded me that whatever I do, I must do it with all my heart as unto him. Even if it is laundry, do it as unto him (see Colossians 3:23). I learned that if no one praises me for my contributions, God is pleased when I render my service unto him or for his glory. So whatever the task, do it unto God and not unto people.

So you see ladies men respond to praise and if you praise him right; you will get an outstanding performance prompted by praise but motivated by love. It is pleasant

13

words that are as honeycombs, sweet to the soul (mind) and health to the bones (see Proverbs 16:24). A good man wants to hear pleasant words, words that will bring ease to his troubled mind and not words of torture and pain (nagging).

My beautiful queens no one wants to be around a nag. In fact, the Bible says that it is better for a man to dwell in the wilderness or desert than with a contentious, nagging, and vexatious woman (see Proverbs 21:19). That is something to think about. If you are nagging your good man, he would rather live in a desert and have peace than to live in a house with a nagging wife. Therefore, **stop nagging him and start bragging on him**.

Nagging does not promote performance. It is praise that promotes performance. Men are goal and performance oriented and when you supply praise, he will always respond. In fact, he will go beyond his and your expectations. Raise the praise!

WORD BUILDERS

Ladies, it is imperative that you work on your vocabulary and learn how your good man responds to the right words spoken to him. There are two words I would like you to add to your vocabulary. They are *compliments* and *thank you*.

Yes, men also like compliments and a simple but sincere "thank you". Compliment him, do not compare him with your sister's or neighbor's husband. The image you are seeing in your sister's husband is him putting his best foot forward. You are not seeing the private struggles and seasons of change it takes to become a good man. You are seeing his "glory" and not his story.

You must purposely acknowledge what your good man does right. He will in response strive to do better, make a difference in the home, and in his relationship with you and the children (if you have any). If he does a good job with taking out the trash without you telling him, praise him in that area. Call him the *Sanitation King* and watch his response.

You may be saying that is not my husband. He never takes out the trash. First, let us remove "you never and you always" out of the vocabulary. Secondly, if you continue to say he never then he won't. Here is a possible approach to getting your good man to take out the trash. "Honey those trash bags are too heavy for me and I believe they will not be a problem for a strong man like you." And before you can complete the statement "would you", he will grab the trash and go down to the curve. Why? Because you acknowledged his strengths and all men like it when you believe he is strong and can do anything.

The other word we mention to add to your vocabulary is "thank you". Thanks or thank you will go a long way. It is sad but even in a love-relationship between a husband and wife the words "thank you" is almost extinct. No one wants to be taken for granted. Whenever appreciation is not shown to the person and what they do; it is interpreted to him or her as "What I do does not matter and neither do I."

So I urge you, say "thank you" to your good man. If he is a stay at home father, thank him for doing such a great job with raising the kids and maintaining a clean house. If he works, thank him for working hard to provide a safe place to live and food to eat. If he helps you clean around the house, thank him for helping you realizing that he does not have to do it. If he is a man of integrity, thank him for being consistent and honest. If he is integral in ministry, thank him for living what he preaches. Just say "thank you". It is just that simple.

Ladies it will be with love and kindness that you will draw your good man. Love is stronger than death and if you love him with your words, you will be amazed at the life that will spring forth in him, your relationship, and all that is connected to him.

LOVE *in* ACTION

● Practice praising what he does well.

● Replace nagging with bragging on him.

● Remember to say "thank you".

● Show appreciation for him and what he does.

QUESTIONS *of the* HEART:

What have I learned from Secret 2 *Praise Him*?

How can I implement this secret beginning today?

NOTES
••••••••••••

CHAPTER THREE

Listen to Him

nother secret I give is to listen to him. For a man, a listening ear is very important. *When a man knows he is being heard and he will not hear of it in the morning; he will share the secrets of his heart.* He will give you the key and access to the secret chambers of his heart.

A VIRTUOUS WOMAN

The Bible says that when you are a virtuous woman your husband will safely trust in you (see Proverbs 31:11). He will safely trust you. Why? Because he believes that you will not use his secrets against him and throw them in his face sixty seconds or six months later. He will trust you because he sees you as a friend and not an enemy.

Ladies, when a man gives you his heart; you have the man. He can give you money and diamonds and not give you his heart. He can even give you great sex and still not give you his heart. *A man's heart is his most valuable asset.* It is in his heart where he is most vulnerable. It is in his heart that he houses his dreams, fears, hopes, disappointments, experiences, memories, hurts, and times of joy. His heart is his treasure chest and only a virtuous woman will be given access.

If you are a woman who has loose lips, a good man will not reveal to you the secrets of his heart. Why? Because he knows that a talebearer reveals secrets but one who is trustworthy and faithful will keep the matter concealed (see Proverbs 11:13). For example, if your good man sees you consistently telling your girlfriends the "dirt" you know about your other girlfriend's man, he will not share with you. In fact, you may have asked him, "Why don't you share with me?" Here is the answer, YOU TALK TOO MUCH! I had to be blunt because if you are going to be successful in your love-relationship, you need the truth. He is thinking it, but he has not come to a place in his heart where he can give voice to his thoughts so I said it for him.

No Condemnation

Listen to him. Listen to him and do not judge him. A good man will not share with you or anyone if he believes that he will be judged by what he shared. He wants to be heard without condemnation. I assure you that if he has come to share with you from his heart; he has already counted up the cost and built up the courage to share with you. Don't blow it with much speaking and a lack of understanding.

Be slow to speak and quick to hear. Listen with your heart. Feel what your man is saying to you. The New Living Translation says that only the LORD can give an understanding wife (see Proverbs 19:14). This is a true statement. Only the Lord can give an understanding wife. Only God can give you a heart of understanding for your good man. Therefore, ask God to give you an understanding heart. And if you listen without condemning him, he will share.

A Sounding Board

Listen to him. Be his sounding board. According to Webster's Dictionary, a sounding board is a person on whom one tests his ideas. A good man wants someone he can tests his ideas, dreams, plans, and aspirations on. If you would be his sounding board, you will be amazed at the creativity that will spring forth by allowing him to test his ideas on you.

Listening to him will allow you to connect to his heart. In fact, listening to him and providing him a sounding board will move him to include you and ask for your input. Meaning, he will ask you questions like, "What do you think about this, or how do you feel about this?"

Ladies your good man wants you to hear him and to be given the opportunity to pour out his heart like water in your presence without criticism. Listen with your heart and not your mind. If he is sharing with you, do not allow your mind to go into overtime to get an answer or proper response. *If you are trying to think of a response, you are not listening.* Sometimes he just wants you to listen and not try to fix him nor the problem he is dealing with. Just listen. Be his sounding board.

LOVE *in* ACTION

- ⊙ Be an empathetic listener.
- ⊙ Listen with the intent to understand him and not to fix him.
- ⊙ Listen and don't throw in his face what he shared with you in a moment of intimacy.
- ⊙ Be his sounding board (Ask him if he has any new ideas, goals, or dreams).

QUESTIONS *of the* HEART:

What did I learn from Secret 3 *Listen to Him*?

How can I implement this secret beginning today?

NOTES
•••••••••••••

CHAPTER FOUR

Give Him Space

"Give him space you say?" Yes, even a good man needs space. Here is a scenario to think about. He goes to work and while there he experiences great pressures. He undergoes mental stress, fights for his position, promotion, and reputation. While fighting, he does not cheat but retains integrity even though his competition fights unfairly. He is tired, frustrated, and has to do it all again tomorrow. In the back of his mind, he is thinking "home sweet home." However when he gets home and stands in the door, he is not greeted warmly. Instead, he is hit in the face with the problems of the household and a long to do list.

Now you tell me, would you want to come home to this house after warring long in the workplace? Of course not, if any thing you will find reasons to work later or find somewhere else to go instead of home.

DOWN TIME

Ladies, your good man does not mind hearing about your day and its events; however, he just doesn't want to hear about it as soon as he arrives home. He needs DOWN TIME. He needs time to unwind and wash away the frustrations and stress of his workday. Whether he is a minister, businessman, or stay at home dad, he must have time to unwind and replenish his soul.

For a good man, DOWN TIME is vital to his productivity, strength, focus, and creativity. If he does not get down time, his productivity will slow down. His strength will decrease. His focus will grow dull and his creativity will be stunted. He will be depleted, all used up. He will not be effective as a husband, lover, father, leader, or as a companion.

He will have nothing to give. He can't give you time because time was not given to him. He can't give you TLC because

TLC was not given to him. He is empty and beaten up by the punches of the workplace and life. He needs down time.

Why down time? I'm glad you asked. Down time will allow him the opportunity to be built up and rise like an edifice higher and higher. His strength will be renewed. His soul will be restored and emotions stabilized. His focus will be clearer and his love for you will be strengthened.

Just a little down time can transform a tired; discouraged man into a confident, strong conqueror ready to face tomorrow and its challenges. He will be your hero and will remember you for saving him from a day of hell on earth. *Even a good man needs to be saved from time to time.*

WAYS TO GIVE HIM SPACE

So you may be asking, "How do I give him space?" Good question. I'm glad you are interested. First, you must set a peaceful atmosphere where he is invited to come in, rest and feel free to be himself. A good man wants to know and feel he can let his guard down at home. He has played the role in the work arena with people who do not even know him. He wants to come home and just be himself.

If you have children, include them in on giving your good man space. How? The next time daddy comes home from a long day instruct the children to greet daddy with a big hug and those three big words "I LOVE YOU". He will be surprised and overtaken with joy because instead of them asking him for something; they made time to love on him. He will appreciate that and later on that night they can ask him for the money (just kidding).

Another way you can give him time to unwind is to have his bath water already drawn at the right temperature or have the shower turned on at the right temperature; which ever he prefers. Play some of his favorite music softly. Light some relaxing aromatherapy candles (if he likes candles) and let him know that tonight you are going to wash his back and all the cares of the day away. He will love that attention. *Even good men like ATTENTION.* Don't let the strength and courage fool you.

Here is something my wife does for me. LaKeida gives me time to unwind by inviting me to lay my head on her lap and reassures me with a soft voice that everything is going to be all right. What an awesome place to be; able to lay your head on the lap of your spouse while she relieves your cares by rubbing your head gently. For me, it is like a calgon moment and I am taken away by every gentle stroke.

Another way I get down time at home is by applying the "*30 minute rule*". Once I arrive home, I greet my wife and after that I get 30 minutes alone by myself. I don't receive phone calls, to-do lists or questions until after my 30 minutes of down time is complete. These 30 minutes alone allow me to unwind and unload the pressures of the workplace so that I don't take them out on my wife. The 30 minute rule protects us from unnecessary, intense fellowships (arguments) and I believe it will work for you.

So there you have it ladies, even though we are different, men have emotions also. Where as you are quick to verbalize what's on your heart with many words, a man internalizes what is on his heart by deep thinking. Bishop Jakes called them "He-Motions." We have emotions just like you. The difference is in our expression of those emotions. Your good man needs down time. He needs time to unwind; time to for himself. He needs the time to unload the stress and pressures of life and download the peace of God into his heart and mind. Give him space.

LOVE *in* ACTION

- ⊙ Recognize his need for down time.
- ⊙ Create an atmosphere where his soul (mind, will, emotions) can rest.
- ⊙ Find ways to make the transition from work to home favorable.
- ⊙ Save your to-do list and challenges of the day for later.
- ⊙ Ask him what he likes and how can you make his down time more enjoyable.
- ⊙ Give him to time to unwind.

QUESTIONS *of the* HEART:

What did I learn from Secret 4 *Give Him Space*?

How can I implement this secret beginning today?

NOTES

•••••••••••••

CHAPTER FIVE

Support Him

One is too small a number to achieve greatness
—JOHN MAXWELL

One is too small a number to achieve greatness. The things God has called and ordained for your good man to accomplish in his lifetime is too great for him to achieve by himself. Even though he may appear to be strong and independent, he needs your support. Every good man, if he is an honest man, will admit that he needs HELP. It is vital that we have a support team around us to assist us in fulfilling our purpose in life.

The Bible records that *two are better than one because they have good reward for their labor* (see Ecclesiastes 4:9). So this tells me that God will never permit you or I to succeed by ourselves. *Success is not a destination but a journey during which great people, resources, and good choices contribute to one's desired outcome.* In your good man's life, you can choose to be an asset or a liability. I believe you have chosen to be an asset by the fact that you purchased this book. Another reason I believe you have chosen to be an asset is that you are woman enough, and humble enough, to admit that you do not know everything but are open to wise counsel to improve your relationship with your good man.

Your good man wants you to support him. In fact, I am going to go further and say he needs your support. He needs someone to assist, help shoulder, advance, stand by, stick up for, encourage, and promote his full potential in reaching his destiny. You as his support must not only be willing to go with him, but you must also be willing to grow with him.

His Interests

One of the ways you can show support to your good man is to share in his interests. What is he interested in? What excites him? What is he most passionate about? What has his attention (besides you)?

When a man is interested in something, his attention is given to the thing that intrigues him. You can play a part in that by taking the time to find out what he is interested in. Whether it is music, sports, money market, historical findings, or even cooking, it will do his heart good to know that his wife is interested in what he is interested in.

You may be saying, "I don't like sports." However, it is not what you like right now but what he likes and finds interesting. When you are supporting someone, you have to lay aside what you feel and consider him and what brings him happiness. Now, I'm not saying go to every football game; however, it will be wise to take as little as five minutes a day and read the sports section of the newspaper and learn the sports jargon. Once you do that you can ask questions about what you do not understand.

Asking questions will be the key in sharing his interests. You may ask a question like, "Did you know that so and so team went to the playoffs?" Now he may already know that information; however, now he knows that you know that information and are interested in what he finds pleasurable. This method can work whether he is interested in cooking or race cars. The objective is to find out what he is interested in and share in that interest. *You do not have to master his interests; just share in them.* Then, you will discover what brings him extra happiness and be able to contribute to his personal pleasure.

BELIEVE IN HIM

Another way you can show support to your good man is to believe in him. Let him know that he is your hero; he is your superman. This sounds simple but for some ladies it is challenging. You have some ladies who believe in their good man but do not say anything. While on the other hand, you have ladies who say that they believe in their good man but their words are not believable and he knows it. Your believing in him and speaking it must go hand in hand; they must agree. Every man wants to know with confidence that the people in his life believe in him and his ability. A good man wants you to know that he is "The Man" and he can do it. He can get the job done.

Your confidence in him encourages him and he is able to draw from his inner strength and do the things he is created to do. He is free to tap into his purpose and maximize his God given potential. He is free to be your hero. So the next time you have an opportunity, tell your good man, "I believe in you." His countenance is going to light up and you will witness a different pep in his step and heighten performances. However, you must not stop with words alone. Yes, the words "I believe in you" are encouraging, but your encouragement must be supported by your actions. You must show him that you believe in him. Remember the old cliché, "Talk is cheap." Men are visual beings. Show him you believe in him.

COVER HIM

Every good man needs to be covered. When I say cover him, I mean pray for him. Prayer, I believe, plays a vital role in the success of your good man and him reaching his destiny. Why pray for him you say? Because praying for him gives you the opportunity to partner with God to see His original plans and purpose accomplished in your good man's life. Truly, as long as he is on this earth, your good man is going to need some *divine* assistance. He will not be able to do it alone. As John Maxwell said, "One is too small a number to achieve greatness." He is going to need help from other supportive people and above all help from God—*divine* assistance. Prayer is the way to give God the legal right and permission to interfere in his affairs and cause his plans to succeed.

Now the question may be, "What exactly do I pray for?" I'm glad you asked. The things that I am going to share are not limited to this list. It is only a guide to help get you started in praying for your good man. You can pray for his vision; pray for his purpose and that he will have an understanding of what it is. Pray for his choices and that he will choose the best in every situation. Pray for his priorities and that he will always put first things first. Also, pray for his relationships and that he will be joined with the right people. Pray for his fears and that he will confront the things he is running from. In addition, pray for his health and that he will make a continuous effort to eat right and be physically fit. Moreover, pray for his integrity and that he deals honestly and speaks the truth in his own heart.

Just simply pray for him. Cover your good man. Invite God to assist him in maximizing his potential and reaching his destiny. Ask for *divine* assistance.

DOMESTIC SUPPORT

Now you may be saying I was with you, but I do not know about this domestic support stuff. Domestic support means simply to clean up. *A good man enjoys a clean and safe environment to come home to.* Yes, I had to say safe because there are some brothers whose environments are not safe to eat, drink, sleep, or breathe in.

Having a clean house does not mean it has to be a perfect house. It is simply an environment that is suitable and proper for the residents to enjoy and live in. Now if you both work, the responsibilities of the house should be shared. My wife and I share the cleaning responsibilities and it does not take away from my manhood. So if he is a good man and I believe he is, he will set aside his ego; pick up a broom and help make a difference in his environment.

The other side of the coin may be that your good man works and you are a domestic engineer (housewife). If this is so, there should be no reason for a brother to come home to a nasty house. The dishes are still in the sink; the beds are not made up; there is no meal prepared and you still have your sleeping clothes on from the night before. Something is wrong with this picture.

You as the housewife play an important role in creating an inviting atmosphere and a clean environment for your good man to come home to. You can accomplish this by setting attainable goals for yourself each day. By setting these goals, you will know what you have to accomplish and you can allocate how much time each goal will take you. After you have accomplished what you planned to do, take the time to celebrate your achievements (no matter how small). The objective is a clean house and not a perfect house. So my queens, do not place yourselves under unnecessary pressure to have a perfect house. It is not a perfect house that a good man wants. He wants a clean house.

Now to my career women, if your schedule and profession does not permit you to clean, HIRE some domestic help. No excuses. Your good man wants a CLEAN house and a safe environment that he can invite his friends to come over and not be ashamed. Just keep it clean!

LOVE *in* ACTION

- Be adaptable.
- Study your good man.
- Share in his interests.
- Believe in him.
- Pray for him (ask for divine assistance).
- Clean up (Strive for a clean house not a perfect house).

QUESTIONS *of the* HEART:

What did I learn from Secret 5 *Support Him*?

How can I implement this secret beginning today?

NOTES
••••••••••••••

CHAPTER SIX
....

Bringing it all together

O k, so you now know the five secrets to keeping a good man. Now what? I am glad you purchased this book and perhaps you may have recommended it to someone else. Thank you. However, reading this book alone is not going to change your love-relationship with your good man. Knowledge alone is not power and neither will it change your life or mine. *It is applied knowledge that produces results.* It is when you and I make a decision to change and apply what we have heard, read, or been taught that we truly change.

Change begins with choice. We can choose to change to get better or worse. It is up to us. *It is the decisions we make that decide our outcomes.* My cousin Amanda often says, "Learn better. Do better." Yes, that is it! Learn better. Do better. Refuse to let this be another book added to your library without making the decision to change. It is when you and I apply what we have knowledge of that truly gives us the power to change. *Change begins with choice and progress is intentional.* Make a decision within yourself that if my love-relationship is going to get better then I must get better.

Don't let this book and its love suggestions become another "to do" list. My objective in sharing these five secrets to keeping a good man was not to give you something else to do on top of all the other million things you are already doing. I wanted to show you that you don't have to reduce yourself to schemes, plots, tricks, love potions, and manipulation to keep a good man. You are better than that and a good man doesn't find those bags of tricks attractive.

You can do this. You can keep your good man. You can win the heart of your good man and experience a lasting connection with him by intentionally applying the five love secrets presented in this book. Wishing and hoping will not change anything. It is your faith with corresponding action that brings about phenomenal results. **If the relationship is worth having, it is worth working on it.**

Let us review the five secrets to keeping a good man once again:

⊙ **Love him:** Show him your love with words and actions. Satisfy him sexually. Show him respect and honor him for the role he plays in your life. Create an environment where he can feel accepted and approved of when he is with you. Be his friend and not his opponent.

⊙ **Praise him:** Celebrate and acknowledge his strengths. Use good words that build him up. Instead of nagging start bragging on him. Tell him thank you for the things he does for you.

⊙ **Listen to him:** Listen without judging him. Listen with the intent to understand him and not fix him. No condemnation. Be his sounding board.

⊙ **Give him space:** Recognize his need for down time. Create an atmosphere where his soul can rest. Ask him what he likes and how can you make his down time more enjoyable. Give him time to unwind. Make it memorable.

⊙ **Support him:** Study your good man. Be adaptable. Share in his interests. Believe in him. Pray for him. Keep the house clean and safe.

NOTES
•••••••••••••

ABOUT THE AUTHOR

FOR OVER TEN YEARS, THIS dynamic, multigifted life changer has been equipping individuals to discover destiny, maximize potential and to use their lives to make an eternal difference in the earth. He is a highly respected preacher, teacher, coach, mentor and a speaker who is known for "*keeping it* real."

Rodney D. Robertson is the founder and CEO of Rodney Robertson Ministries and New Life Christian Center. He is also an entrepreneur, publisher, and author. He is the author of two life-changing books, *After the Mistake, Then What?* and *Free to Be Me!* He is married to his beautiful wife, LaKeida Robertson. They reside in Louisiana.

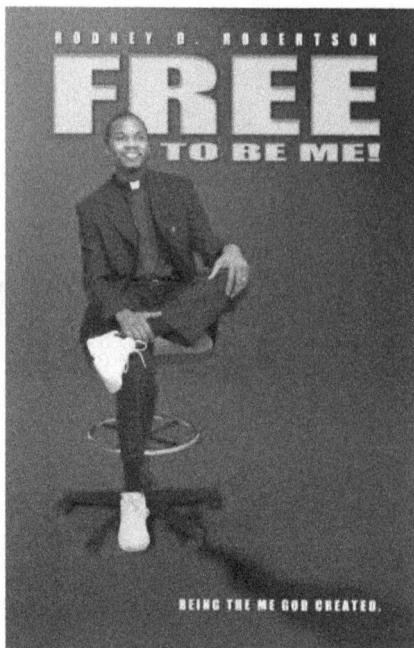

ISBN: 1-594673-72-1, Paperback

Inside *Free to Be Me*, Rodney will show you how to be the best you that God created. He will also provide you with freedom keys that will empower you to live a life free of other people's opinion of you. Discover the joy of being you, a priceless original, and not a cheap imitation.

AVAILABLE AT THE FOLLOWING WEBSITES:

www.xulonpress.com

www.rodneyrobertson.org

www.amazon.com

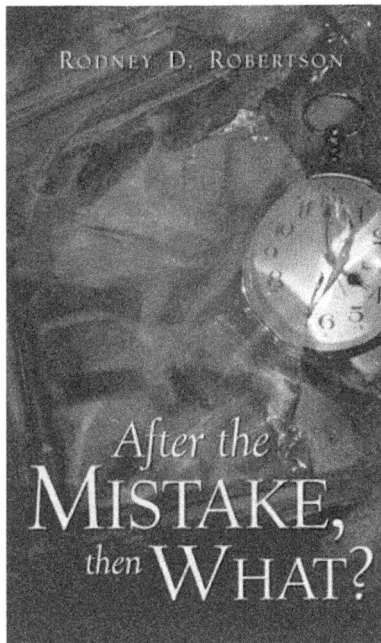

ISBN: 1-59160780-9, Paperback

Inside this life changing book, Rodney wants you to know that you are not the mistake you made. You can get up again and there is life after the mistake. You no longer have to walk in condemnation and guilt. *After the Mistake, Then What*, has an answer for your dilemma. Read and be liberated from the guilt of your past. **You are not the mistake you made!**

AVAILABLE AT THE FOLLOWING WEBSITES:

www.xulonpress.com
www.rodneyrobertson.org
www.amazon.com

CONTACT
INFORMATION

WE HOPED THAT YOU HAVE enjoyed this book by Rodney Robertson. If you would like to receive additional information about the author or to book the author for a speaking engagement, please send correspondence to the following address:

Rodney Robertson Ministries (RRM)
PO Box 74610 - Baton Rouge, LA 70874
www.rodneyrobertson.org

SERVICES RENDERED
BY RODNEY ROBERTSON:

SEMINARS:

HEART2HEART MARRIAGE SEMINAR:
Equipping individuals within a marriage to build
a healthy and lasting relationship.

DISCOVERING DESTINY SEMINAR:
Equipping and inspiring individuals to discover destiny
and maximize potential.

BACK2PRAYER SEMINAR:
Equipping and empowering individuals to operate
in their authority in prayer.

WINNING WITH WISDOM SEMINAR:
Equipping individuals to operate in divine wisdom
so that they can win in life.

Additional copies of this book are available from
Rodney Robertson Ministries and online at www.
rodneyrobertson.org.

RODNEY ROBERTSON MINISTRIES
Attn: Products Department
PO Box 74610
Baton Rouge, LA 70874

www.ingramcontent.com/pod-product-compliance
Lightning Source LLC
Chambersburg PA
CBHW060147050426

42448CB00010B/2337